HOLLY ALEXANDER

BEGINNING

MAGIC MONEY

A COURSE IN CREATING ABUNDANCE

BOOK ONE

Published by Magic Money Books

Copyright 2017 © Magic Money Books

All rights reserved. No part of this book may be reproduced or transmitted in any form or by any means, electronic or mechanical, including photocopying, recording or by any information storage and retrieval system without written permission of the publisher, except for the inclusion of brief quotations in a review.

Digital ISBN: 978-0-9980731-8-7

Paperback ISBN: 978-0-9980731-9-4

HOLLY ALEXANDER

BEGINNING
MAGIC
MONEY

---•---

A COURSE IN
CREATING
ABUNDANCE

---•---

BOOK ONE

YOU'RE INVITED

I would like to personally invite you to the Magic Money Books community at Facebook.com/groups/MagicMoneyBooks where you can join in on the magic! You'll find daily support, affirmations, and inspiration from like-minded individuals on their own magic money journey.

I'd also love to hear from you personally! You can connect with me through email at Holly@MagicMoneyBooks.com. I look forward to connecting and hearing about your magic money journey soon!

TABLE OF CONTENTS

Chapter One:
Magic Money 1

Chapter Two:
The Beginning of Your
Magic Money Life 11

Chapter Three:
A Magic Money Mindset 21

Chapter Four:
Magic Money Maximization 33

Chapter Five:
Your Magic Money Experiment 59

Chapter Six:
Consistency is Magic Money Gold 71

Gratitude 81

Who is Holly 83

Dear Reader,

Welcome to *Beginning Magic Money*, the first in a three-book series. This is a book series I've been excited, and incredibly hesitant, to write for about ten years. Let me explain.

During most of my adult life, I've practiced and practically perfected the prosperity principles I discovered by reading the classic works of Catherine Ponder, Florence Scovel Shinn, Emmet Fox, and the more present-day and recent works of Pam Grout, Rhonda Byrne, Shakti Gawain, Dr. Wayne Dyer, and Mike Dooley.

I have thoroughly enjoyed manifesting money in tiny and massive amounts, customers and clients by referral and out of thin air, as well as free and discounted goods and services from expected and unexpected places for the past twenty years.

It seems to me there is a huge disconnect when the word "manifesting" is used. While I don't believe I can sit in my living room (or in the front seat of my car), and wish something into being, I believe in using my mind to bring about what I want. I use it to visualize my goals, raise my vibration to "joy," set intentions, and most importantly, have an expectation that all I need will come to me at the exact moment I need it.

In my personal and business life, it has been easier to talk to some people about "out there" concepts like the Law of Attraction, setting intentions, allowing results, and "what you think about you bring about." Others have resisted, and rightly so because for some it is seemingly impractical to do anything other than work hard and wait a reasonable amount of time to achieve their goals.

I don't believe life should be tough, hard-fought, or a difficult struggle. I'm living proof that a consistent daily practice or two, combined with unwavering faith, right alongside some serious mad respect for the money that comes into my life, can go a long way toward making the path to abundance, prosperity, and success faster and simpler than anyone might believe!

So, if you watched or read *The Secret* with crossed arms and a skeptical eye, this book is for you. If you've read *The Dynamic Law of Prosperity* with an open mind, but it was too religious or preachy for you, I get it. If you've wanted for longer than you can remember to be more prosperous and abundant (read: richer than you are or have ever been), I understand. You'll find practical applications outlined that will make sense and take virtually no extra time out of your day to perform. And, you'll get results—most of the time, the first results show up within 24 hours. And, when you commit to a continuous practice, the magic money will not only continue to come, the amounts will be bigger and bigger.

I'm taking the "woo woo" out of manifesting and prosperity in my quest to help you prove to yourself, once and for all, that money—and life—can be easier and more effortless than you ever thought possible.

Holly Alexander

INTRODUCTION

I was introduced to *Unity Church* while I was attending *Marble Collegiate Church* in New York City in my early twenties. Both churches, while different in their foundations, shared positive messages of hope and possibility. My favorite sermon by then Executive Minister Arthur Caliandro was *You Can Do It, So Do It*. I still have the cassette tape of the sermon I purchased immediately after his message almost 25 years ago.

INTRODUCTION

I was a foster kid who had also spent some time in a children's home during my teen years. I had endured years of physical and mental abuse at the hands of my advanced-degree professional parents, who simultaneously instilled in me that I was brilliant and capable *and* completely worthless and hopeless.

This dichotomy resulted in a seemingly insurmountable challenge: to feel good about myself, to do something with my life, and make a difference while I'm on this planet. I didn't have low self-esteem; I had *no* self-esteem and thought and acted accordingly. When I was exposed to personal development and the possibility I could do something with my life, achieve the vision for my life of my choosing—one that would mean something, I got a tiny bit excited way down deep inside. My first goal wasn't to have a healthy self-esteem, it was to *not* have bad self-esteem. If I couldn't feel good, at least perhaps I would be able to stop feeling awful. It didn't take long, only a decade or so for the effects of my self-help practices to take hold. (Smile.)

In addition to reading his books, I attended virtually every Tony Robbins seminar and listened to every tape program he offered. I discovered there were not only beliefs I could adopt about myself that were positive; there were actions I could take to improve my life. Practical, daily action steps I could do and when I did them they worked. When I got complacent or cocky and stopped doing them, lo and behold, they stopped working.

This book is full of the actions I've been taking for years, actions I've turned into habits that have served me, and those around me, well.

In fact, years ago I had a small group of friends and clients begin doing their own Magic Money experiments. These "Experimenters" experienced an increase in income, but they also lost weight, manifested new, loving relationships, got promotions, started successful businesses, bought new homes, and so much more.

The primary theme of the Magic Money Philosophy is this:

Focus the great energy of your thinking on abundance, and treat all you receive with respect, and you will have abundance—despite what is happening around you.

If you're ready to get on the path of receiving your own Magic Money and lots *lots* more, then turn the page.

Chapter One

MAGIC MONEY

***Magic Money** is money and the incredible abundance you attract into your life through expected and unexpected channels through the practice of the Magic Money Philosophy.*

For most of my adult life, I've been able to manifest just about whatever my heart desires. In addition to money, I've had a steady stream of customers, clients, and work. I've received discounted and free "stuff," as well as the cars, homes, and vacations I want, gifts of services, clothing, expensive shoes, jewelry, and more.

All of the above have come to me because I've done just a few simple and easy things every single day.

You probably picked up this book because you know, deep down, there must be an easier and better way. You want something more, including more money, and you want less of the stress and struggle that comes with not having enough.

I completely understand. I didn't come from money, and I don't have an advanced degree or formal education ensuring my personal, professional, or financial success.

My ability to manifest not only things I wanted, but also unlimited amounts of money, is based on simple, easy and almost effortless daily prosperity practices, combined with an unwavering positive attitude, and a dogged work ethic. I call the magic combination of these daily actions "prosperity practices for practical people." And they yield magical results, including, yes, *magic money*.

I didn't learn these techniques from my parents or a mentor who held my hand and provided guidance. I discovered what worked—and what didn't!—through several years of trial and error. I read lots of books, listened to lots of audio programs, and even attended a seminar (or twelve). I watched with keen interest how my wealthier friends and sometimes bosses handled and talked about money. I made mental notes and journal entries. It wasn't very long before I had the beginnings of something pretty amazing.

So did my closest friends!

Those closest to me saw first-hand literal manifestations of exactly what I wanted right when I wanted it. They saw me say, *I'd love to have X happen,* then stare with amazement when my cell phone rang with that exact result. Finally, they've watched as I've said *I need $8,000 to make that happen* or *I'll only do it for X price,* only to have the money show up "magically" or the seller to meet my price (in retail and real estate).

Of course, after more than a few things happened, they asked how I do it. And, of course, I shared with them some of what I was doing. I'm perceived as a rational person, I've been told, and they were trying to reconcile how a practical, non-woo-woo person seemed to not only practice but get results that could only be described as 'out there.' Wouldn't you know, once they tried some of my "secret" strategies, they got results, too.

My dear friend Bill realized his two-seater pickup truck wasn't ideal for chauffeuring around potential homebuyers in his real estate business. Within ten days, he received enough to pay cash for a foreign four door sedan. One of my best girlfriends, Bobbi Jo, was laid off from her job as a country club interior designer when the development sold out. I convinced her not to panic, and instead practice my Magic Money Philosophy. She launched her own interior design business and had two six-figure clients in the first month. One of those clients is now her husband; they just celebrated their ten-year anniversary!

I have not only shared my practices with my very closest friends, but I've shared it with small groups of other people who got wind of what I was doing. Throughout the years as people have questioned my "luck" and witnessed my success, I've gone "open kimono" with a few select people. These are my Experimenters, and you'll meet some more of them later.

I believe, no *I know*, there is a harder path and an easier path. Through trial and error, I've discovered the inner and outer thoughts and action that qualify as the simpler path. Who doesn't want to know about, and take the easier path? I know you do, or you wouldn't be reading this book!

No doubt you picked up this book because (a) I know you would love more money and abundance in your life (who wouldn't?) and (b) you're a practical, hard-working person who would like the pragmatic formula that makes sense *and works.*

My Magic Money Philosophy is based on a simple principle: what you put out comes back to you. Said another way, what you radiate is what you attract and how you treat money is how money treats you. Until you begin to intentionally and consistently tell the "Powers that Be" (whatever you call it: God, the Universe, Universal Intelligence, or even your subconscious mind) what you want to have, do, be, create, and manifest into your life, and do the *actions* that work, you will get what you've been getting (good, bad or indifferent).

In short, you must:

Focus the great energy of your thinking on abundance, and treat all you receive with respect, and you will have abundance—despite what is happening around you.

I'll be talking at length about this in this series of short books; however, what *magic money* comes down to, in its most basic and purest form is this: mixed intentions cause mixed results and one clear intention causes one clear result.

You must set one clear intention to get one clear result.

Such as *I desire to have an abundance of money.* Everything I do is toward that one clear intention.

Sometimes we feel confident and not only put out confident thoughts and energy, we act with confidence. In return, we experience great results. Other times we doubt ourselves, what is possible, and act accordingly. It's no surprise we get awful results. By engaging in daily practices founded upon a positive thought and practical action process, you begin to get results immediately—usually within 24 hours—and will continue to get consistent results the longer you do this process. It doesn't matter what's been going on in your bank account, life in general, or business up to this point, with these simple practices, you can reverse and/or accelerate your results starting today.

If you want to fully and successfully participate in the Magic Money Philosophy, you must decide right now that you're going to:

- Take control of what you think, say, and do with money, **and**
- suspend disbelief; **and**
- let go of every belief you have that money must come to you through specific channels {i.e., through your job/career}; **and**
- think and speak about money in a positive way; **and**
- allow money to come to you from anywhere at any time; **and**
- believe that there's more than enough for you now and henceforth forever, **and**
- an abundance of everything you need is indeed on its way to you *right now*.

Isn't it time for you to be open to receive all that you want out of life, including money and an abundance of anything and everything you want and need? I think so!

Above is the mindset side of the Magic Money Philosophy. There is also the practical action side of the Magic Money Philosophy. You must also decide right now to:

- be respectful toward your money at all times, **and**
- spend your money with intention and purpose, **and**
- save your money with intention and purpose, **and**
- have fun with your money on purpose, **and**
- grow your money with intention and purpose.

Being respectful, intentional, and purposeful in your treatment of each cent you receive, by whatever means, will cause money to be attracted to you from all directions. The money that comes to you will stay with you and grow, the money you spend will be returned to you multiplied. You won't have to spend as much money when you purchase goods and services, and you'll receive bonuses, discounts, and even find money wherever you go.

What I'm describing might sound too good to be true, and I promise you it isn't. I will share every nook and cranny of my Magic Money Philosophy to you.

In this book, *Beginning Magic Money*, I will give you a fresh look at money and abundance as a whole. If you've been in a state of struggle and lack for as long as you can remember, jumping right into advanced techniques will only serve to frustrate you. I know from experience a gradual increase in prosperity consciousness has the best chance of "sticking," and will serve you just as it has served me.

In the next book, *Advanced Magic Money*, you will learn advanced money manifesting and multiplication strategies. As your consciousness increases, so will your ability to earn, receive, and increase your wealth and abundance.

By the time you are ready for *Magic Money Mastery* the sky will be the limit to what you can manifest, when, and how. I'll help get you ready for a life of unlimited magic money and wealth and abundance.

You might be wondering why I don't just have one book instead of three. The answer is quite simple, and I alluded to it above: too much too soon equates to failure. Trying to make huge leaps and bounds in your beliefs and actions can, due to lack of results, lead to frustration, discouragement, and eventually, giving up. I know because I've done it myself, and those with whom I have worked closely have experienced setbacks and failed results for multiple reasons (which I will share with you in detail so you can avoid them).

If you're like many people I know, you've tried manifesting and failed. You've watched *The Secret,* said affirmations, and visualized yourself silly. (Me, too.) But I'm a pragmatist at heart, and once I combined practical practices with some of the more esoteric prosperity practices, that's when the real magic (money) happened.

I promise I understand exactly where you're coming from, have been there myself, gotten out of it and helped others do the same. I will hold your hand, give you a concrete plan and steps, show you that you are a powerful creator, and exactly how to put it all together.

For you to make steady progress, you must be purposeful with your magic money practices. If that sounds fabulous to you, then kindly turn the page and let's begin!

Chapter Two

THE BEGINNING OF YOUR MAGIC MONEY LIFE

It is the rare person who can go from barely subsisting to becoming a multimillionaire in three easy steps, all within 30 days. Thus the reason I started the Magic Money Philosophy series with *Beginning Magic Money*.

What is possible for you is an abundance of happiness, success, and yes, money. The Magic Money Philosophy isn't all about the money. It *is* about abundance in every area of one's life. In fact, I believe money (like everything) is energy, and can, and should, be used as a tool to help us to live the life we want to live. We should have an abundance of money, as well as an abundance of everything else we want and need.

My very favorite thing to do with my money is to *give it away*. I do my very best to do good things with the abundance I have in my life. I also love to travel in style, provide a wonderful life for my family, and experience everything life has to offer.

Having an abundance of everything you need and want, including money, is fabulous for a few reasons – and I'm sure you'll agree with every last one of them:

- Be your best, most generous and beautiful self.

- Be your most creative and contributing self.

- Be the best parent, son or daughter, friend, neighbor, and professional possible.

Aren't you a happier, nicer, less-stressed person when you have everything you need? Aren't you more generous, friendly, and joyful? I know I am, and the Experimenters mentioned in the Introduction vigorously agreed when I posed that question to them. Since introducing the Magic Money Philosophy into their lives, if there's anything they can agree on it's that more abundance equals less of what they don't want and much more of what they do.

With enough magic money, you are free to live the life you may have only dreamed about before today. There are two equally important elements to the Magic Money Philosophy. Intelligently and purposely applied, you can go from straining and striving to abundant and thriving.

What you might have been doing wrong, or said a better way, what you might've been doing right, is just degrees away from what would take you from climbing the stairs with the wrong shoes and a heavy pack on your back to taking the express elevator straight to the top.

I'm going to break each element down into logical, practical ideas and action steps that should make complete sense to you. Not only that, you will want to start doing them right away. If I've written this first book correctly, you're already fired up and chomping at the bit for me to *get down to it*. So let's, shall we?

Julia and Richard

People who have an abundance of money find, manifest, and make money with a seeming relative ease. Their *set point* is "an abundance of money." A money set point is similar to a temperature set point. If your thermostat is set at 72 degrees, when you get cold, the heater is going to turn on. When it gets too hot, the air conditioning will kick on and immediately start cooling the place off. The goal of both settings is to return to the set point. What's interesting about our money mindset set point is that it is, at least until we take control of it, run by our subconscious minds.

If you are always struggling with money, a bit of reflection might reveal that while you sometimes have more money than others, you consistently return to your set point. When there's an absolute lack of money, you get nervous and do some things to earn more or spend less – or both. When you have more money, you might tend to be less intentional, or perhaps "buy something now before all of the money is gone." This cycle will repeat itself for your entire life until you become conscious and make changes.

Julia, one of my Experimenters, reported that when she used to get her annual bonus, it was almost always gone within a few days. She felt compelled to spend recklessly (although she didn't consider it reckless at the time) until there were only a few hundred dollars left. Having those several extra thousand dollars would give her a feeling of freedom and excitement, but also stress and pressure. Because she wasn't comfortable with feeling freedom and excitement with money, she literally "got rid of it" as soon as she could. Then the stress would lessen, and she would go back to business as usual until the next year.

Richard, another Experimenter, had spent most of his life hoarding money, fearful he will spend his money "wrong," and as a result, accumulated quite a bit of wealth. Yet, he lived in sparse conditions, preventing himself from experiencing the joy his wealth could bring to him and those he loves.

Neither Julia nor Richard would be where they are today if they didn't take a hard look at their patterns with money, identify their set point, and make small yet significant changes in their thoughts, words, and behaviors.

Because you're reading this book, I know at least one thing about you: you want more money. And now you know you have a set point that is probably (definitely) keeping you in the same place you've been, maybe for decades. I'm excited for what comes next for you because I had a similar experience with money until I got control of my mindset and started to maximize my money.

Beginning Magic Money Mindset

You're here because money gives you anxiety. You live in constant fear you either don't have enough or you at some point, next week or someday, won't have enough. You might lie awake at night and worry about not having enough money, or you constantly speak about how you can't afford what you want or even what you need (like groceries or paying your electric bill).

Dave Ramsey talks about baby steps when it comes to taking control of one's money. While I haven't participated in his program, I have read quite a bit about it. I love the term "baby steps" when it comes to taking control of, shifting, and expanding one's money mindset.

Trying to make a giant leap from where you are to where you want to be can be a huge mistake. Big jumps in consciousness do happen, but they are exceedingly rare. In fact, if you've tried to expand your consciousness in various ways before and failed, you're not alone.

Taking small steps to expand your mindset will ensure that you will permanently change your set point.

Expanding your mindset is not unlike training for an endurance run such as a marathon. If you've never run before, you wouldn't just decide to run the local marathon on Sunday. You would begin a training program that would most likely have you alternate running with walking until you'd built up your endurance. You might not be able to run a mile today, but in six months or a year, you could easily run an entire marathon with proper training. *And love every moment of it.*

Beginning Magic Money is the part of the program where you begin to expand your overall prosperity consciousness in small but not insignificant ways. Permanently changing what you believe about money, how you think about it, and what you believe about it will simply mean you have more of it. In fact, you'll always have exactly what you need when you need it, with plenty left over.

Money is like air, I promise you! You don't worry that the last breath you took is going to be the last of the air available to you, or that you might run out of air to breath. You just breathe. It's natural, you do it, and you don't think about it.

To get to the point where money is like air *for you*, you must make some changes—some permanent, lasting, and enjoyable changes.

Beginning Magic Money Maximization

In addition to your mindset, how you maximize your money is crucial, too. If you struggle with money, it is because you don't treat it with the respect it deserves, therefore it is not drawn to you. You might be repelling money—and that's such a bummer! There is more than enough money for you, when you know how to treat the money you receive, starting today.

When you receive money, do you already know what you're going to do with it, or do you just "play it by ear?" I would guess you don't already know, or you wouldn't be in search of more of it. You would be at a point where you always have more than what you need, whenever you need it.

If you live, at least a little, with a YOLO (you only live once) philosophy, you might be tempted to splurge when you should save. You might take your money life "one day at a time." While each feels good in their own way, they also come with a side of guilt, and a huge helping of long-term stress.

In addition to thinking, speaking and believing differently, and dare I say better, about money, once you begin to receive, spend, save, and grow your money with the respect it deserves, you will find money comes to you, from multiple sources, in increasing amounts, *on a daily basis.*

Read that paragraph again, because it is important. I didn't say you had to work harder. In fact, I didn't say anything about work at all. Having more money, having *magic money*, is sometimes connected to work, and lots of the time it isn't. But I'm getting ahead of myself.

I want you to start getting, keeping, and attracting more money today, and that means it's time for …

Chapter Three:

A MAGIC MONEY MINDSET

If the thought of "money is like air" is a lot to take in, I get it. Many of the original Experimenters recoiled at the idea of attracting magic money and manifesting abundance. To them, it sounded big and complicated. It also sounded *impossible.* I showed them how to gradually increase their money mindset until they reached the "manifesting money is easy" stage.

Because the only way I got to a place of unlimited magic money in my life was by taking tiny steps and having incremental growth, I introduced them to changes in what they thought and did that would incrementally increase not only what they thought could happen, it also influenced what did happen.

Look, your world, your financial world, won't change until you change. Your life today reflects the person you are and have been, up until now. You take small steps and keep taking them, and ultimately, you will arrive at your intended destination. The little things you do begin to yield little results, and eventually your results, the amounts of magic money that come to you, get bigger and bigger and bigger.

The Magic Money Philosophy consists of seven distinct steps, and I've already shared them with you. This time, I'm going to break them down, one-by-one.

Number One: **Take control of what you think, say, and do with money.**

This step is a big one, that's why it holds the first position. When you think about money smile, because *money is good!* When you speak about money, say awesome things such as *Money is awesome! I love money and money loves me! I always have more than enough money. Money comes to me, in increasing amounts, every single day.*

Before you get all, *I do not love money, and this lady is crazy!* Relax, Sparky. No, you probably don't love money like you love a good cheeseburger, or your wife, or kids or anything like that (although there's nothing wrong with that!).

You love money because of all the great things is allows you to have, do, be, give, and create during this magical ride we call life. Everything you do, every single day, is supported in some way by money. Money paid for the door you open and close to leave and return home. It pays for the cell service you need to text your kids to tell them you love them. It was used to make the roads you use to go places. Money is around us everywhere, and I think it's amazing!

You want money to love you because when money loves you, it comes to you in spades. Every. Single. Day.

You can't live as though you're already receiving an unending stream of magic money until you are. Doesn't it make sense, then, that you do with your money is just as critical to your long-term wealth and abundance as what you think and say about your money?

Number Two: **Suspend disbelief.**

If you look at an expensive watch, car, or home and can't conceive of the fact that you, too, could have them (if you wanted to), you must suspend that disbelief, because *anything you want can be yours.* It just might take some time, so be prepared to take the time it takes. Keep your negative belief suspended until then, while you're replacing it with a better one.

If you think those who own expensive items and have an abundance of money are bad in some way, you won't end up staying in the flow of magic money (if you manage to get there in the first place). Money doesn't make someone good or bad. I believe money, like alcohol, makes someone more of who they are—if someone is a good person, more money will help them be better and do more good. If you're a good person, having more money will allow you to do more good in this world, for yourself and others. Make sense?

It is, in fact, it is wealthy individuals who fund charities and social programs in which they believe. You can do more good in the world with the wise use of your magic money than you can from staying in a state of lack and limitation. But first, you must let go of any belief you have that separates you from your magic money! Which leads us to…

Number Three: **Let go of every belief you have that money must come to you through specific channels (i.e., through your job/career, an individual or entity, etc.).**

Hey, guess what? Money can come to you in so many ways, it's crazy good. You can: find money (ever found $20 in your pocket? Or change on the street?), be left with money (you could have a rich relative you know or don't know about), get more than you thought was coming (tax refund, anyone?), or unexpectedly get to pay less (unexpected discounts or rebates are everywhere). If you think money can only come to you through a specific channel, such as your job, you are not right! Replace your belief that money only comes from specific places you've already identified, and replace it with the belief money is coming to you from multiple sources, on a continuous basis, and you're ready and willing to be pleasantly surprised at any moment. **Smile**.

Number Four: Think and speak about money in a positive way.

Money is energy and responds to what you think about it and say about it. If you believe money is evil, or the people who have it are evil, then logically you won't be open to having copious amounts of it. I will go much deeper about your money self-talk in *Magic Money Mastery.* For now, see Number One for suggestions.

Number Five: Allow money to come to you from anywhere at any time.

Slightly different from Number Three, this is the state of *allowing* money to flow to you from wherever it feels like coming. Does it matter if you get a check from the company you work for, or someone leaves a big bag of money on your doorstep? I didn't think so, and I'm open to both of those possibilities (and an unlimited number of others) myself. I'm unconcerned about where the money comes from, and it's perfectly fine if I receive a huge deposit into my bank account while I'm sleeping. I'm suggesting you get okay with this, too! I, myself, am open to "doorstep money presents" and have a couple of stories I'll share in a later book.

Number Six: **Believe that there's more than enough for you now and henceforth forever.**

More "money is like air" here ... Haven't your needs always been met? Don't all the bills eventually get paid, and at some point, you get or have what you need? That isn't going to stop, in fact, the more you embrace the concept that there's more than enough, the more there shall be.

Number Seven: **An abundance of everything you need is indeed on its way to you right now.**

Take a deep breath and *know* today is the first day you have more than enough of what you need. From now until forever, every single one of your needs is met, your bills are paid, and *even cooler than that*, anything you decide you want is on its way to you the minute you decide you want it.

Isn't it time for you to be open to receive all that you want out of life, including money and an abundance of anything and everything you want and need? I think so! No, I *know* so! Working through each of the above steps will ensure you have a steady stream of magic money and an abundance of everything else flowing to you unendingly.

When you can embrace, and execute the above seven steps, you will be fully in the flow state of receiving magic money. Would you like an easy way to do just that? I thought you would. In case you're intrigued, I'll share more about them in more detail in *Magic Money Mastery*.

For now, here are four magical Magic Money Mindset Action Steps that will get those results mentioned above showing up within 24 hours … and beyond:

1. Take responsibility for your life and everything in it.

What you radiate is what you attract. The way to radiate on the super high magic money frequency is to own every good thing about your life, and every not-so-good thing, and be perfectly okay with it. If your life rocks or sucks in any way, own it. From here on out, recognize you have chosen each one of your circumstances, and take back your power by deciding to choose differently, with intention and purpose, to create a life that's better than ever before. If you dislike any part of your life, that's quite okay because it's going to change for the better and PDQ (pretty darn quick)!

Focus instead on all of the goodness that surrounds you, and be grateful for it. More on that in a minute. But first…

2. Stop complaining, criticizing, and finding fault.

No more bitching, complaining, moaning, or nit-picking. Remember when your mom used to say, *If you don't have something nice to say, don't say anything?* Have you heard *If you cannot be kind, please be quiet?* Same idea. Instead, be a goodfinder. If there's someone who is being rude, be grateful it isn't you. Be thankful for the reminder of what it feels like to be on the receiving end *and* be extra careful to be gracious and kind. If you must offer "constructive criticism," come from the place of offering information the other party might want.

3. Keep a Magic Money Journal.

Write down everything you have to be grateful for, and all of the evidence of abundance that exists in your life right now. Keep a running list of all of the money you receive, and where it comes from. While you're upping your good finding game, keep a list of the good you see. You might not live in the home of your dreams, but do you have a warm, comfortable bed to sleep in? That's abundance, my friend (a large percentage of people in the world can't say the same). Do you have someone to call and tell when you receive unexpected magic money? Friends are an example of abundance. Can you read this sentence? You have eyes that can see and to have clear vision is a true blessing. Do you have any money in a bank account, investment account, back pocket, or wallet? Write it all down! Write down not 5, not 10, but 25 or 50 (or more!) things right now that are evidence you live in a world of abundance. (Go ahead, I'll wait.)

4. Record your results.

Do each of the seven steps, combined with being a good-finder, keeping your lips zipped when you feel like complaining, and writing down your manifestations and blessings in your Magic Money Journal, and whoa Nelly, watch what happens! You'll feel happier, more positive, joyful, and lighter. Money loves the new you and will flow to you in ways you can't even imagine.

Remember this: there are zero coincidences. You can, will, and should see results almost immediately. Big and little good things that happen are not luck, a fluke, or chance. When you look for little bits (and huge chunks) of evidence, you will find them. Every little thing that happens from this point forward, every additional unexpected dollar, discount, or gift can, and should, grow and reinforce your belief in yourself and the Magic Money Philosophy. Yes, it's true, you do contain the power within you to activate magic money and unlimited abundance.

One final thought on the magic money mindset: You must choose to believe that every good thing you see, and everything that happens, and every dollar that comes to you is a clear sign you are on the right track, you are magical and you are attracting more and more magic money every single day. These instances of manifesting money are evidence, and you must be sure to note them in your Magic Money Journal.

The flip side of the magic money mindset coin is magic money maximization. Think you're ready? I know I'm ready to share. Turn the page …

Chapter Four

MAGIC MONEY MAXIMIZATION

A vibrant magic money mindset creates half of a solid foundation for becoming a top-notch magic money manifestor. The other side is how you treat money because how you treat money is how money treats you. Together, they activate the magic money flow and catapult you to the next level.

If you resent rich and wealthy people, that's the same as resenting money. Ever been around someone who resents you? Of course, you have, we all have. Want to be around them all the time? Nope. Neither spending money frivolously or hoarding money works well, either.

Frivolity is a sign you're uncomfortable with money, and money scatters around nervous energy. Hoarding is a sign of fear, and money flows away from fear.

You must show money the respect it deserves. The more respect you show it, the more it comes to you. You must also spend, save, and grow your money with intention and purpose.

But what does that mean, Holly? Well, I'm going to tell you, and I think you're going to love it.

You absolutely must be respectful toward your money at all times. The word respect is *the condition of being esteemed or honored, and respectful as showing deference.* I treat money as an extension of myself, and I treat myself with respect. Because you're a human being walking this planet, you deserve respect. The same goes with anything you own, do, or have contact with—including money.

Here are a few beginning magic money steps you can take when handling your money:

- **Keep your money organized.** Neatly keep your money in your wallet or money clip. I put mine in order of currency. I straighten out the corners and face each bill in the same direction. I rarely crumple up a dollar and put it in a pocket (but it has happened, don't get me wrong … mostly before I adopted the Magic Money Philosophy). A messy wallet can contribute to a messy financial life. A well-organized wallet shows respect for yourself and your money.

- **Keep spare change in a bowl until you have enough to make a decent-sized deposit.** Feng shui experts advise you to put a bowl of change in the wealth Bagua of your home and office. I keep bowls of change in a few different places in my home, and when the bowls fill up, I roll the change and deposit it into my savings account. It is pretty to look at, yet doesn't earn interest in my bowl. Eventually, you want your money making money (in the form of interest in this case).

- **Carry a fair amount of cash.** I usually have at least $200 on me at all times. I'll share a bit later what I do with it, but here's what you need to know right now: having a nice amount of organized cash on me helps me to feel abundant. It allows me to give a generous tip to a valet, or give money to someone when they need it. It also helps you to avoid saying the words, *I don't have any cash* right about the time having some cash would be super helpful.

I've combined spend, save, and grow your money with intention and purpose, because you will take in each amount of money that comes to you and allocate it in the way you choose in advance.

I'm going to be explain in more depth later, but for the time being this is for informational purposes only (in other words, don't *do* anything differently yet—I'll tell you when).

A Sneak Peek into Advanced Magic Money

Part of showing respect for money is being purposeful in how you handle it. I advise you to identify a percentage that feels right to you, and for each dollar, pound, or Franc that comes to you, you'll allocate it to an account you've set up for each purpose. Stay with me; it isn't at all complicated.

You most likely have a deposit account that receives all of your money. That is your *spending* account. In addition to that account, eventually you will need to have the following accounts: Giving, Saving, Fun, and (if you're self-employed) Taxes.

Note: You won't need a Debt account, you'll just make lots (and lots and lots) of payments toward any debt you have, until it is, indeed, all paid off. I'll explain more about that shortly.

Let's discuss each one in brief detail, and we'll for sure go much deeper in *Advanced Magic Money*:

- **Giving:** Wealth begins in your mind, and the truly rich give money away. Since you're on your way to having an abundance of magic money, by default makes you rich (even if right now, today, it truly is only in your mind)! The very first thing you can do to start the flow of more money coming into your life is to plan to give away a percentage of every dollar you make. In short, you'll identify an organization you wish to benefit, and make them the recipient of your giving percentage. Giving teaches your subconscious mind you have more than enough to give to others (and you do).

- **Saving:** wealthy people also have what some call a "war chest" or amount of reserve capital available if needed. I like to think of my savings as "opportunity money" and I've also heard the term "freedom fund," It's called this because it's there if or when I might need it for something awesome. Or once you've accumulated enough, you get to the point where you *never have to do anything you don't want to do ever again*. I've rarely used my savings account, and there's zero judgment if you ever need to use it! Sometimes unexpected things happen, and it's good to know you're got it covered. Ultimately, your Savings account will spill into your investment account (discussed in depth in *Advanced Magic Money*).

- **Debt:** if you're currently in debt, a portion of each dollar you receive goes to pay it off—*after* you've given and saved!

- **Fun:** Magic Money is fun, and you need to have "fun dates," or Artist's Dates (as Julia Cameron called them in *The Artist's Way*). Putting aside a portion of your income for fun makes the connection with your subconscious mind that money equals fun. Your subconscious mind is the silent yet *most powerful player* in the Magic Money game, and it's important to keep this player happy.

- **Taxes (if you're self-employed):** check with your accountant to determine the percentage you need to set aside for your taxes.

When you receive money, you'll deposit it into your *spending* account. Next, you'll transfer the percentage you've pre-determined for each account and move the money. Whatever is left is used for any bills you have and for anything else you'd like to use it.

But, as I said, don't start doing anything quite yet. Just take a deep breath and keep reading.

My First Magic Money Maximization

I didn't have a philosophy when I first started. I had read about tithing (which is a religious practice used by many of the world's religions), and of course, you can't read a book even as simple as *Personal Finance for Dummies* without learning about the act of saving.

While I'm more spiritual than religious, I decided to give tithing a try along with the act of saving. My numbers back then were quite small.

At the time, I was making about $185 a week after taxes, had $700 in credit card debt (which might as well have been a million dollars), no savings, and no other assets. I didn't even really know about investing back then, but this was nearly thirty years ago so don't be too hard on me.

The next check I received, I gave 10%, or $18.50, and moved $18.50 into my savings account. I remember it distinctly because it was the first time I had ever tithed or given money away, and it was also the first time I had ever put money into savings. I was maybe all of 21 years old and had been on my own for several years. Both concepts were new to me, and what did I know? Practically nothing. I took the advice I heard and read, and more than two decades later, I can say engaging in these practices is one of the top three best things I have ever done!

After giving and saving, I had $148 left for the week. I had enough to pay my rent, buy food, and pay for public transportation. I was excited to have some money in savings but was nervous about how I was going to make it through an entire week with the $40 or so dollars I had left after I had paid my bills.

Oh yes, and my credit card bill was due again in about three weeks. I wasn't sure how I was going to pay that bill on time, and I made a conscious decision to *not* worry about it but trusting what I had read about the benefits of tithing and giving. I also started saying affirmations when I felt fearful about money. I'll talk more about affirmations and what to say when you talk to yourself in *Advanced Magic Money*.

Within a couple of days, I was at dinner with my boyfriend Michael, his best friend, Steven, and Steven's wife, Elizabeth. Elizabeth just "happened to be" looking for a temp for her office who could type fast and was proficient in *Microsoft Word on the Mac*. My best typing test was 120 wpm with zero errors, so on the first count, I was a shoe-in. I knew a Mac was a computer, but I had no idea what Microsoft Word was. But when Elizabeth asked me if I was up for the job, considering it paid a whopping $18 an hour, which would almost triple my take-home pay, I said, *You bet.*

(Then I called my wealthy friend Stephanie, who was many years older than I was, and had a computer at home—a huge deal back in those days – and asked her if she knew what *Microsoft Word on the Mac* was. She did and offered to let me come and learn on her setup. I learned enough over the next three days to convincingly do the job.)

It wasn't long before I had paid off my debt, and was convinced giving and saving were a terrific idea. I am sure you can see why!

Was the new job, and income, a coincidence? I'm not sure. But I do know I had been in my financial predicament, which was rapidly going from bad to worse until I intentionally changed my trajectory.

Wait, is it Tithing or Giving?

Just as you might have questions about tithing, I have a couple of thoughts about it as well. As I said, I'm not a particularly religious person. But I do believe in a higher power, and for this conversation, I will refer to it as the Universe.

My giving journey began because I started tithing. As I've shared with others my Magic Money Philosophy, many of them have recoiled in horror at the mention of tithing because they aren't religious or worse, have had a negative religious or church experience. Something I knew could and would work wonders wasn't even something they would entertain because of the religious connotation. Rats.

I used my favorite reference (Google, of course) to find a short definition of tithing, and here's what I found: *tithing is a one-tenth part of something, paid as a contribution to a religious organization or compulsory tax to the government.*

That doesn't sound awesome to me, and if I were just reading that definition for the first time back when I first started, it would have sent me running (and probably screaming) in the opposite direction. There are scriptural references in the New Testament, and most religions talk about and encourage tithing. If you are a religious person, then you might already tithe, or have tithed in the past. But if you're still a little skeptical, don't give up on this quite yet.

Stay with me; I promise the results you'll get will be worth it!

I did some thinking and upon reflection, realized tithing was just another word for giving. I searched for something that could help me create a bridge and help people keep an open mind. Catherine Ponder has an affirmation: *My giving makes me rich.* I think Mrs. Ponder would agree with me that it doesn't matter what you call it, either tithing or giving, it is a good practice.

Whatever you call it, do it! Here's why:

The act of giving reinforces to your subconscious mind that you do have more than enough. If you can easily part with 10% (or even 1%) of your income, then you can easily (and quickly) manifest more to replace it. Right? When it becomes a matter of habit, rather than something you must convince yourself to do, you step fully into the magic of *Magic Money*. Once you've gotten to the place where an automatic 10% flows out of your account (just imagine tipping the valet an extra $10), you will know you've activated a channel of magic money right to your wallet.

But before I get too ahead of myself, there's something else I must share with you.

I'm going to be completely honest with you, mostly because I have no reason not to *and* I recognize transparency on my part will provide both hope and information you definitely need.

I haven't always stayed on the program and in the magic. My first husband, Sam, about lost his mind when I tried to tell him about tithing. He was vehemently against it, and so for a time, I didn't do it. Immediately after we got married, he was the sole breadwinner for about a year. *That year was the hardest, most stressful, and poorest of my life.* Because he made the money, he directed the spending. And he definitely had not been introduced to the law of attraction, tithing, saving, or an abundance mindset.

We were miles apart in our thinking, and while I had the answers at my fingertips (because before we married, I had been practicing magic money for about three years), I deferred to Sam. I shushed my intuition and my knowledge, and therefore I suffered. *We* suffered. Unnecessarily, I might add.

When I got tired enough of the suffering, I picked up one of my favorite books from before I had met him (there's a list at the back of this book), and make the life-changing decision to resume tithing. Sam was gone a lot with his job, and that meant I oversaw the finances. I knew tithing and saving would work, and I figured our financial situation couldn't get any worse. By this point, we had spent our way through most of my savings, and we were well past my line of feeling comfortable. While "ask for forgiveness, not permission" isn't necessarily the best personal philosophy, that's what I decided to do.

Within a few days, I got a call from someone I had previously done some work for, who asked if I was willing to do a bit of traveling, I would earn several thousand dollars in a week's time. (Thank you, 7th-grade typing class.)

That money gave us some breathing room, and I recommitted to my giving and saving practice. Once we got into the flow again, I didn't look back. I also stayed in charge of the finances!

And you'd have thought I would've learned my lesson and stayed with it forever and ever until the end of time, right? Well, no. Not exactly.

What's unfortunate is it took several periods of lack and limitation to convince me to commit to forever until the end of time to *give* and *save*. When I have, in the past, stopped giving, I've also stopped saving. Eventually, my savings account would be empty—and I'd have to start over.

Before you even get started I have one important piece of advice for you: once you start, keep going (and you won't have to start over).

Magic Money Distribution

As you can probably guess from my example, above, I suggest a 10% contribution into each account. In this example, we'll use the round number of $1,000:

Giving: $100

Saving: $100

Fun: $100

Debt: $100

That leaves you with $600. Use the remaining money to pay bills, buy groceries, and put gas in your car. You might notice it doesn't leave you with much, but I promise you if you stick with it, you will see results. You will turn on the flow of magic money. Within a short time, you'll notice that your income will increase, and your bills will stay the same or decrease. You will have released the magic, and now you're on the receiving end of an abundance of magic money, and so much more.

You might be doing the math and thinking *No way can I live on 60%. Can. Not.* I get it! There's magic in this, which is the fun part. But we're going to get into what seems like an ice-cold pool very slowly.

If 10% is just way too much right now, I understand. Trust me when I say you want to get to a place where you're in a real state of abundance, and magic money maximization is the fastest and easiest path to making that happen.

You might need to start at 5% or even 1%, and that's perfectly fine. With 1% to each account, that is $10 for each account, leaving you with $960. A contribution of 5%, or $50, leaves you with $800. Whatever percentage you choose, make a commitment to stay engaged in the process until you start to see results. Once that happens, you won't ever want to stop—this I can guarantee you!

You might need to economize or budget to stick to the program. Take a lunch from home, ride the bus, or minimizing your cable bill might be an option. If up to this point you've been living at more than 100% of your income, you will have to earn the trust of your money and yourself.

It is worth it to work both sides of the magic money coin by getting your mindset and your magic money in order.

I don't like the word budget any more than the next guy, but let's face it: you won't engage any magic until you get honest with yourself. There's a lot about the Magic Money Philosophy that is fun, and once you're fully in it, you won't have to budget for the most part. But I am a very pragmatic person, and you can't expect to do what you've always done and get something different as a result.

Regardless of the percentage you choose, as I've said, once you've made the decision you must commit 100%. No matter what, you'll allocate your money immediately as soon as you receive it. You might be tempted to keep it in your *spending* account, but don't. Allocate that money just as quickly as your little fingers can log onto Chase.com. You're staying in the flow of abundance, and you don't want to interrupt the flow of magic money, right? (Trust me on this one.)

When to Use Your Savings, and Spend that Fun Money!

You have these two fantastic accounts that are accumulating money from the very first day. If you call your savings account your "freedom fund" because of the fabulous feeling having an abundance of money in reserve feels, you'll feel equally as delighted about the money in your "fun fund."

You might be wondering when it's okay to use those monies. Your savings account should remain untouched, while you use the money in your fun account with all of joy and enthusiasm you can muster—to have fun!

Your Savings Account is Your Freedom Fund

The purpose of the savings account is to provide long-term financial freedom. You should only dip into it in the event of a bona fide emergency. If you can avoid using your savings with some strategic budgeting or the occasional float (until the money starts freely flowing in), that's for the best. You might find, however, on occasion, you need new tires or have an unexpected medical bill that needs immediate attention. Fearlessly use your savings to keep you out of debt and in good standing with your providers and creditors. Once you have committed to the process and stepped fully into the flow, you will find your savings account isn't needed and continues to grow and grow.

Having an abundance of money I don't *need* has given me a few different freedoms I didn't originally expect. I have remained self-employed for all my adult life. I navigated the major stressors and costs associated with a divorce (attorneys, therapists, moving, buying a new car), and even buy a new house with a substantial down payment.

I have seen people cope with illness or other life challenges (such as the death of a spouse, breast cancer, and getting laid off), and each time they have had one other major stressor: *money*. My savings has always given me the knowledge that in the event something happened to me and I was unable to work, there was enough in reserve to take care of my basic needs. Eventually, by the time I became a single mom, I didn't miss a beat: I knew I had enough to take care of myself and my daughter no matter what happened. Not forever, but for long enough I could figure out something without stress, strain, or worry. And without a significant downsizing of our lifestyle, either.

Multiple Streams of Magic Money Income

This book isn't about "making more money" per se, but I feel compelled to mention one strategy I have employed over and over throughout my working life, and I think it might be a light bulb moment for you (it was for me). You have probably heard of multiple streams of income, yet when people talk about it, they don't really explain what it means. I not only thought it was a good idea to create multiple streams of income, but I also worked to create multiple streams of income that cover more than what I need to live every month.

My first business allowed me to create leveraged, repeat income through customers' purchase of products, and I receive an override on the people who built businesses in my organization. I haven't worked that business in over a decade, yet without fail, once a month I receive a direct deposit that covers a fair amount of my monthly living expenses. I don't do anything except continue to use the products each month. Without continuing to focus on it, the income stream I had initially built did eventually get smaller and smaller but has stayed steady at a few thousand dollars a month for many years.

Once I discovered I could make money without trading time for money, I have kept an eye out for other opportunities to create more for myself and over the past two and a half decades have done just that.

If you have one stream of income, that's awesome! You might want to keep your main hustle while you keep your antennas up for ways to create some side hustle money that can eventually match or exceed what you're already earning.

Your Fun Account is Strictly for FUN!

I love putting money into my fun account. I usually have my eye on a spa day or a fun summer excursion with the family. Right now, I'm planning a three-month European vacation! I thoroughly enjoy the process of saving up for it rather than going into debt.

If you're just starting out, a fancy pants vacation or a new car paid for in cash might be a bit much for you to handle and I understand! I remember when I felt like a big spender when I could buy *two* drinks at the Borders Café instead of just one for my daughter and me to share.

Identify something wonderful you would like to do with your fun money, and when the time comes, fork over the cash so you can enjoy every moment of your fun.

Imagine being able to pay cash for each new and exciting thing you bring into your life or do for joy. I don't know about you, but I like my money to make money as opposed to earning more interest I must pay back over time. I much prefer a bit (or a lot!) of delayed gratification to minimize my stress and maximize my fun.

I'm saving up for something special, and I've been saving for about two years. I'll be saving for another year or so (we're talking a 7-figure purchase), yet when we finally make the purchase, my husband and I will not have a large monthly payment that is half principal and half interest – we will have 100% ownership. I get giddy every time I think about it!

But this isn't about my giddiness; it's about *yours*. I want you to have lots of fun, joy, and giddiness in your life, and I want you to have some as soon as today. You might choose to open a fun account, throw some money in there and decide to get a massage or manicure or pedicure right now (which might be a very good idea to get you on the magic money train right away). Today I'm going to visit one of my favorite stores to buy a pair of wedge sandals I've had my eye on—I was just waiting for a check to arrive so I would have some money for just that purpose in my fun account. Or you could decide you want to save up for an Audi R8 or to buy a home with cash. I have two fun accounts, one for the more instant gratification things like the sandals and manicures, and a separate one for the big purchase I'm looking to make.

It's entirely up to you what you do with your fun money, and that is entirely the point. It's for *fun* and only for fun. I don't give many directives, but listen up because I'm going to give one now: you can never use your fun money for something that doesn't give you joy.

Now, you might also be a single mom (or dad), and it would give you joy to buy little Johnny a new pair of shoes or some football pads for his uniform. Fine. But I have a good reason for recommending a fun account to be used solely for your good pleasure.

You might be wondering why I'm not recommending you pay off all your debt before accumulating, and spending, money for *fun*.

It's purely psychological, my friend. All budget and no play makes your lizard brain pissed off, and rightly so. Part of the reason money gives most people so much stress is not only because there never seems to be enough, and money is also supposed to be very serious. We're so busy trying to make money and figure out how to spend it "just right" so we have just enough, "enough" or even a bit more than enough. We miss the opportunity to think about it as a tool we can use to make our lives, and the lives of others so much better.

When you set aside, and use, a portion of your income, earnings, manifestations, gifts, and money you find to have fun, your subconscious mind equates money to being fun! The bonus is it will work on your behalf to get more of it. We are wired for fun, frivolity, and even some occasional instant gratification. Shift your brain from thinking "money equals pain" to "money equals all sorts of shenanigans" and you will be able to walk with delight as it flows into your life as never before!

Make sure you hear me now: Using your fun money for fun will work in your favor to help you get, keep, and have more money both now—*and over the course of the rest of your life.*

Fun doesn't have to be a 5-star trip to a foreign land. No, fun can be something simple, like a movie *with popcorn and candy and soda*— or a massage, or even a picnic in the park. I remember when my weekly fun outing was a trip to the bookstore with my daughter. I didn't yet have enough money to buy the magazines I loved to read (and would much rather have read with a cup of tea on my couch). But the bookstores had them! I thought it was rude to show up and not buy anything, so we spent our fun money on one, and eventually two, cups of something delightful from the café. We would go there on Saturday or Sunday morning and spend a few hours browsing the shelves, reading books and magazines (and sometimes the music selection). Then we would head home for a nap – also fun, but totally free (and delicious).

It does not matter *what* you use your fun money to do or buy; it simply matters that you use it for something that brings you joy or do something enjoyable. Like having a savings account with some cash reserve, the process of using your fun money reinforces to your subconscious mind that money is *good*, money is *positive*, and therefore it will jump on the magic money bandwagon with you.

Congratulations—you have learned the basics of the *Magic Money Philosophy*. Now the time has come to put it into practice and begin to create your own stream of magic money! It's time for you to take what you now know and turn it into something you do. Are you ready? Let's get this party started!

Chapter Five

YOUR MAGIC MONEY EXPERIMENT

*K*nowing what to do and doing it are two entirely different things. As I've mentioned, I have practiced the Magic Money Philosophy like a boss at times, and at others, not so much. Without a doubt, I can say a commitment to a consistent practice is anyone's best bet in the long term.

But you're not me, and if I were you, I might still be a tiny bit skeptical. Or, perhaps, you are down with this theory in theory, but you will believe it when you see it. And you want to see if it will work for you.

Fair enough. Whatever you're thinking right now, the only way to know if it works is to see if it works, right? Right!

For the next 30 days, you're going to do your first Magic Money Experiment.

Many of my Experimenters found attracting magic money and manifesting for themselves sounded big and complicated, yet doing the same for someone else or a cause they believed in was something they could easily do. To that end, I suggest you identify an amount of money you would most like to manifest or attract for someone you love or a cause close to your heart.

It costs $50,000 to build a home for a grateful family with Rebuilding Together. A donation of $1,000 can feed and clothe a foster child for a month in most states in the U.S. There are countless legitimate charities or organizations you can land your focus on and support.

Or, you might have a friend or relative dealing with a life-threatening illness and additional monies could lead to peace of mind as they focus on their treatment.

Your First Magic Money Experiment

The first part of your first experiment is to identify the amount of money you want to provide to the organization or person of your choice.

Now write that number down and set your intention that amount of money will show up at the perfect time, in the perfect way. (In case you're wondering what "set your intention means," stay with me. I'll circle back to it shortly.)

There are four additional action steps in your first experiment, and they are simpler than you might think. For the next 30 days, at least, do these four things:

One. **Take responsibility for your life and everything in it.**

You are not a victim. There is no one to blame for anything. The choices you've made up until today have brought you to where you are today, good, bad, or indifferent.

Ultimately, there is no good or bad—*it just is*. Accept every aspect of your life, including and perhaps especially, your financial situation, just as it is.

Look, you may have been a victim of someone else's naughty or plain old evil behavior. Nothing you can do about it! Just look at it, think to yourself, *That's interesting*. And then get on with your day. Ultimately, there's nothing else you can do, is there?

Write this Statement of Responsibility in your Magic Money Journal: *I take full responsibility for my life and everything in it.*

Two. **Stop complaining, bemoaning, or bellyaching.**

No more criticizing. Not even a tiny bit of gossiping, back-fence talking, or scuttlebutt discussing. If you don't have anything nice to say, *say nothing*. If you're having a tough day, or someone has been particularly unkind to you, resist the urge to light them on fire and repeat (to yourself and anyone who asks): *Everything is working out for my highest good, and I can't wait to see what happens next!*

Three. **Grab a blank journal and christen it your Magic Money Journal.**

In your journal, keep a running list of everything you are grateful for or could be grateful for if you were paying closer attention. You live in a world of massive abundance, and your job is to notice it, notate it, and be grateful for it. Make it a point to add to it every day, at least once a day. Magic Money flows to the person who lives in a constant state of gratitude for gratitude is just another way to describe the state of abundance. Write as many things down as you can every day.

Whenever you feel doubt, lack, or fear, write at least five things down. And walk around your home, touch the objects you own and be thankful for them.

Magic Money Accelerator: Write thank you notes! The fastest way to "turn the Titanic around" is to make a list of anyone you can possibly think of who has done anything even remotely nice for you. Your neighbor gave you a cup of sugar, you heard from a long-lost client and got to spend some time catching up, you received some unexpected money—all good reasons to bust out a thank you note.

Four. Watch for, and record your results.

Receive unexpected income for work you've done? Write that down. Get a new client or customer "out of the blue?" Put it on the list.

An unexpected check arrives in the mail? Write it down. You find money on the sidewalk? Yup, that's not only a positive result, *it is also a sign you are on the right track*. It is the Universe giving you a nod and a wink. Smile to yourself, and write it in your Magic Money Journal.

That's it. That's your First Magic Money Experiment. At the end of thirty days, you should have a notebook with pages slap full of things for which you are grateful. This is your first list of magic money manifestations. Let me point out to you that this is but a teeny tiny list of what can and will ultimately show up for you over time.

If you can keep going to sixty or ninety days, you'll probably have used up more than one journal!

You'll notice I didn't suggest you *do* anything different with your money. While I've told you about the process of allocating your money into different accounts, don't engage in the practice until your Second Magic Money Experiment. You will find it in *Advanced Magic Money*. Let me remind you it is important to get your thoughts right before you take any outward action. Small steps, remember?

Yes, you could read *Advanced Magic Money* and do "all of the things." And you would probably get results so fast your head would spin. But again, if you're like most people (and me), you want to wade into the freezing pool water one inch at a time to make sure I know what I'm talking about.

Alright, let's get back to that woo-woo term I used a bit earlier …

Setting Your Intention

Setting your intention for something may sound like a big deal, or frankly something that tree huggers and bark eaters do. I've found it to be just about the easiest thing I do (well, breathing might be easier).

Setting your intention is another way of saying making an ask, or simply, asking.

I use phrases such as, *It would great if this happened* or *Wouldn't it be nice if* or *I'm gonna need this to show up for me.*

There are two basic steps:

1. Think it or Set it … and forget it
2. Receive it

The only thing in the physical world I could think of that easily equates to setting an intention (which can be considered metaphysical or spiritual, depending on how you look at it) is ordering from Amazon.

I need a food scale. I go to Amazon, select the food scale I like, click "buy now" and (because I'm a Prime Member), the scale shows up in exactly two days.

I don't worry that my order wasn't received and check back a dozen times for the status. I order and forget about it until the nice FEDEX man bangs on my door to let me know he's left a package. In this case, the package is my scale.

Setting your intention is a lot like ordering from Amazon, except you don't have to have a credit card on file.

At first, you'll wonder if it's that easy and I can promise you it is. The more you practice it, the better you'll get at it.

You can build your muscle by intending to see a car you'd like to own, and eventually, you'll intend to own it and you will!

But like I said earlier, if you just intend to own a brand-new Tesla and you haven't already built your intention muscles, you're most likely going to fail.

Start with something small. I started with *I find money everywhere I go*. Finding spare change is something I've done my entire life. I wanted to increase the number of times, so one of my first intentions was to find money everywhere I go, and every day. It worked! To this day, I absolutely find change, and sometimes dollar bills, everywhere, I can't *not* find it! I can't leave my house to take out the garbage that I don't find random change in the driveway. I visited someone's house for the first time yesterday, and lo and behold, picked up a few coins off the floor and handed them to my host. My family just laughs (a little at me, mostly with glee) because, on a recent mall outing, I found thirty-one cents after we parked and were walking to Starbucks. One our way back to the car, same little stretch of concrete in the aisle where we parked, another quarter. It isn't a lot, but it's *every single time I leave my house. Every day. Without fail.* Sometimes I even find it in the gym where I work out!

Author's note: During the editing phase of this book, I re-read this passage. Then went to the gym. Fifty-seven cents *on the treadmill*. I can't make this stuff up!

I'm sure you can see why I suggest you adopt the same or similar belief and set that same intention:

I find money everywhere I go.

After you've been finding money for a while, you'll want to expand your belief and intention.

Once I had "finding money" handled, I decided to move up to *I receive money every day.* Now, I receive a direct deposit into one of my accounts every single day. Yesterday, it was $8.58 from something I had sold online. The day before it was $90 from one source, and $3,000 from another. Most of the time, I simply don't know where the money is coming from, and I don't worry about it. I always have an abundance of money coming to me, from multiple sources, on a continuous basis.

And so can you.

Remember, every single great thing that happens to you is a sign from the Universe you're on the right track. The money that comes to you, the discounts you receive, unexpected raises, and random $20 bills you find in your coat pocket are confirmation your experiment is working. By keeping track of every one of them, by collecting the data, it will add up to incontrovertible evidence you should keep going.

Are You Ready for What's Next?

Be sure to complete at least thirty days of the first magic money experiment before you move on. You might be wondering how you'll know it's time to move on to *Advanced Magic Money*. Here's how you'll know:

One. A positive outlook and attitude is your default setting. You rarely complain about anything, and even when things go wrong, you believe they contain within them the seeds of something awesome.

Two. You feel optimistic about your future. You feel like, maybe for the first time, your struggle has come to an end.

Three. Your life is reflecting your new positive outlook back to you. You see abundance everywhere you go, and you are grateful for all of it.

Four. You see inklings of how powerful you truly are, and you receive money from unexpected places, and find money in unexpected spaces—just about every day.

When these four are true, it is time for you to move on to *Advanced Magic Money*. I'll be waiting for you there!

But before we both go, I have a few more words you'll want to take in…

Chapter Six

CONSISTENCY IS MAGIC MONEY GOLD

Trying to stick to a program forever is tough! In the past, I've been on a diet and just when I was *almost* at my goal weight, something happened. Once, it was double pneumonia. Another time, I had an emergency surgery that left me unable to work, workout, or watch what I ate for a couple of months. Thankfully, I was at a point where I had fully stepped into the flow of Magic Money so I could focus on getting well. All the while, all my needs were met.

My point is: right now, you may be 100% committed to practicing the Magic Money Philosophy and at some point, that number might drop to 70% or even 30%, or maybe even 0%. And that's okay, *mostly*.

I can almost promise you one of two things are going to happen, and heck, they *both* might happen.

You'll get in the flow, pay off your debt, have a big bunch of money in your freedom fund, be saving toward that big fun you have in mind, and be earning and receiving more than you ever have, more than you need. You either decide to or a little bit over time, stop practicing the Magic Money Philosophy.

Or.

Something happens to knock you off course, you abandon the practice for one reason or another, and suddenly you find yourself right back where you started.

How do I know this? Ahem, well, yup, I've been through them all.

I've been "off the sauce" more than a few times, for reasons I shared at the beginning of this book, and I can promise you I won't ever stray from my practices again. Because I know they work, because I don't really like to work hard, and because I don't want to break the stream of magic money! In the past, I've gotten too big for my britches. I convinced myself I had mastered the craft, so I could stop giving. I figured I didn't need to write those four and five figure tithing checks, I'd just hang on to the money for myself. I had enough in savings, so I could just spend the money, almost as fast as it came in, on whatever I wanted.

Big mistakes, all of them. *Huge.*

But I'm not alone. My former assistant, Sheila, worked for my family for several years. She saw first-hand the Magic Money Philosophy in action, and she was grateful I took her under my wing and got her started on her path to wealth and abundance.

But my family relocated, she found other work and even relocated herself. She has always been very close to my daughter, but we had lost touch for a few years while she was traveling overseas. Recently, my daughter was talking to Sheila, who asked to speak to me. When we got on the phone, she said, *Reconnecting with your daughter reminded me I haven't been practicing my Magic Money. So I started saying my affirmations, sent out my first tithe in forever, and made a donation. Within 24 hours, I got a raise, the person in front of me at Chick-fil-A paid my bill, and I got a gift certificate for a massage from a friend. I can't believe I ever stopped! I won't stop again!*

I consider myself a slow learner at times, and unfortunately, I have to learn some lessons several times. I don't want you to suffer the same consequences. I've gotten complacent, thinking the flow wouldn't stop even if I didn't keep up "my end of the bargain." I have given in to fear, mistakenly thinking if I held on to the money I had I would be okay. What has struck me and stayed with me is the fact I have always prospered and had an abundance when I allowed money to freely flow from me and to me. The faster I've given, saved, and enjoyed my fun money, the faster and easier more and more money has flowed to me.

I wouldn't dare stop my magic money practices, even though I no longer "need" them ... I simply don't want to halt the magic! I've learned, through trial and error (and needless suffering) what happens when I take a break from the magic money practices—they take a break from me!

But it's not only me. My Experimenters have had to learn some valuable lessons themselves about the power of the Magic Money Philosophy.

Remember Julia? She got off to a brilliant start by changing her thoughts, words, and actions around money. She adopted a positive mental attitude and immediately started making more sales and earning more money. She seemed to have a new, fun result every day, and within a few months had accumulated more money than she'd ever had in her possession in her whole life. So what did she do? What you might be tempted to do in the same situation: she got complacent and stopped doing what worked.

She started paying for her friends' lunches and drinks. She stopped making a list of her manifestations. Eventually, she lost the momentum she had worked so hard to gain and started to, once again, feel a tremendous amount of fear around money. Thinking her initial success was "too good to be true," she became very discouraged.

I ran into her, quite by chance, and asked how she was doing. She sheepishly admitted *I am kind of right back where I started.* I laughed out loud, not *at* her, but out of full recognition: I had been there myself (and not just once)! I spent a few minutes sharing with her my roller coaster of learning, and she felt better. She also felt encouraged to begin again—and wouldn't you know within 24 hours, the results have started to happen again!

The good news is your abundance is on the other side of your intention! It is just waiting for you to wave the checkered flag signifying it is a-okay to show up. So, on the off chance you stop doing your Magic Money actions, and the flow seems to turn off, I promise it will only last until you start them up again.

I want to share a little more of Richard's story with you, too. You'll remember he was very reticent to spend any money at all, so while he had accumulated a significant stash of cash, he rarely treated himself or his wife to *anything*. They lived in the house Richard grew up in and inherited in his 20s, he drove a ten-year-old car with more than 150,000 miles (as did his wife), and they never took vacations.

Just like I recommend taking consistent tiny steps when it comes to expanding one's money consciousness, I also suggested Richard get used to the idea of spending money. He didn't need to make an intention to receive more money. Although, check it out, kids, that's exactly what happened when he loosened the wallet strings! Instead of *always* looking for a bargain, I challenged him to buy what he wanted regardless of whether it was on sale or not. Instead of brewing his coffee at home, I encouraged him to go to Starbucks and buy the coffee of the person behind him in line.

He took my advice and immediately got out of his comfort zone. At Starbucks, he gave $20 to the cashier and sat and watched as his $20 bought drinks for a few people who came behind him (all while staying anonymous). He's always wanted to go on an Alaskan cruise but felt it wouldn't be a "wise" way to spend his money. He went ahead and booked the trip and started to get excited about it. He told me *Every time I spent the money, I had a moment of tightness in my chest. But then I saw how appreciative others were just for me buying them a $3 coffee! And my wife, she is so excited to go on the cruise. It's been so long since I've seen her so happy and excited.*

But here's the best part: the very day he started these practices, he received a raise. A whopping twenty percent raise! This is particularly interesting timing because his company had been on a hiring, promotion, and raise freeze for the past several years. That evening, he took his wife out for a steak dinner at a 5-star restaurant and tipped the waiter 20%. As they were about to leave, the restaurant brought each of them a $50 gift card to use the next time. The next day, he called me with all of the news and concluded by saying *I've spent my entire life afraid to spend any "unnecessary" funds, thinking I was doing the prudent thing. Little did I know I was missing out on so much joy, and also the abundance that flows back in response to my joy and generosity. You can bet I won't waste one more minute!*

In the past decade, I'm happy to report Richard and his wife bought a beautiful home, brand new cars, and traveled the world, first class. He has continued to practice Magic Money and enjoyed every moment. When I told him I was writing this book, he said, *I'm so glad! I can't wait to give copies to my friends and family. They think I've just been lucky, but they have no idea how lucky I've been and why. I'm looking forward to sharing the gift of Magic Money.*

I hope you are, too!

I hope you have enjoyed *Beginning Magic Money!* When you complete your first Magic

Money Experiment, grab a copy of *Advanced Magic Money* and take your abundance and prosperity up a notch!

GRATITUDE

A huge bucket of thanks to my Experimenters and Magic Money Practitioners! Thank you for validating my process. Wishing you a lifetime of magic money and an abundance of every wonderful thing!

WHO IS HOLLY

Holly Alexander is the author of the three-book series: *Magic Money:* A Course in Creating Abundance. She's a serial entrepreneur, multiple-business owner, philanthropist, wife, mom, avid traveler, reader, and explorer.

She believes you can have, do, and be everything you want to have, do, and be when you treat life and money with the respect they deserve. You can find out more at MagicMoneyBooks.com.

GRAB ALL OF THE MAGIC MONEY BOOKS!

Made in the USA
Middletown, DE
21 September 2018